ROMAN LONDON

ROMAN LONDON
Alan Sorrell

ARCO   New York

TO ELIZABETH WITH LOVE

Published by ARCO PUBLISHING COMPANY, Inc.
219 Park Avenue South, New York, N.Y. 10003
First published in USA 1969
Copyright © Alan Sorrell 1969
All Rights Reserved
Library of Congress Catalog Number 69–12148
ARCO Catalog Number 668–01853–4
Made and printed in Denmark by
F. E. Bording Ltd, Copenhagen

CONTENTS

THE ILLUSTRATIONS

The author's reconstructions are indicated in Roman type

A great gulf of time separates Roman London from the twentieth century, but there can be no doubt that we have a stronger feeling of affinity with this ancient past than with the later Saxon or Medieval times. It may well be that after two devastating wars and social upheavals which have destroyed an established system, if not a culture, we can now appreciate sympathetically the stresses which were endured by the Roman upholders of a precarious world order, whose frontiers, harried by barbarian hordes, were perhaps less vulnerable than was its internal economy. Since we can, instinctively, identify ourselves with these Romano-Britons more easily than with the remoter people of succeeding ages we therefore seek to learn more about them: who they were, how they lived, and especially how their city must have appeared in its days of activity and splendour.

We know exactly the extent of Londinium, and the sites of some of its important buildings. The fort can now, thanks to post-war excavation, be established at Cripplegate—curiously sited for defence when compared with the Tower of London, its military successor. We know something of the street plan, and where the great trunk roads debouched from the towered city-gateways. The bridge was 100 yards east of the present London Bridge. Cemeteries have been plotted outside the walls. All this, and much more, we know, but why, it may be asked, was the city built in this particular locality which has evidently proved to be so appropriate that there has never been any attempt to rebuild it elsewhere? The name Londinium is the Latinised form of the Celtic Londinos, a hypothetical personal name, formed from Londos, meaning 'fierce'. It might be assumed that a Celtic name implies a Celtic foundation, but archaeological opinion is firmly against this assumption, chiefly because of the very small amount of pre-Roman fragmentary remains which have been found on the site. No structural remains of any kind have been unearthed, and this is not surprising since only timber and wattle buildings can be envisaged. In fact a few potsherds only have come to light, and, as it has been established that similar types were manufactured after the coming of the Romans, their presence proves nothing. The Celtic name is thought by some scholars to be an instance of the Roman habit of using native names for their own foundations. It certainly has always been a peculiar indication of imperialist arrogance, this naming of cities and settle-

1 Bronze head of the Emperor Hadrian

9

2 The 'London Jug', inscribed 'At London by the temple of Isis', c. A.D. 50–100.

ments in the language of the conquered and displaced peoples: Ottawa and Kalgoorlie, for instance, will come to mind. But nothing can be proved or disproved. It may be said that Londinium came into being because its site fulfilled all the conditions necessary for a trading port linked with the continent and serving the whole of Britain—that is, Britain under a strong unified rule which could safeguard as well as make use of such a focal point set deep in the land. The Thames was then, as it is today, the natural entrance to Britain, and for continental trade. The city stood at the head of the tidal flood (which today reaches Teddington) where areas of gravel came down to the water's edge and provided a firm well-drained building site and the lowest point at which the river could be bridged. Londinium was open to the south, and protected to the north by rising land covered with a thick oak forest, impenetrable except by the great trunk roads which were presently to be driven through it.

Two low hillocks, or knolls, not more than 50 feet above river level, marked the eastern and western sections of the site. Leadenhall Market now covers the eastern hill, whilst St Paul's Cathedral stands on the western. Between these two knolls flowed the Walbrook. Further to the east were two hillocks where now stand the Tower of London and the Mint, the latter outside the city proper. The site may be simply described as a gravel island, bisected by the north–south axial line of the valley of the Walbrook, sloping down to the river on the south, to the Fleet river on the west, to the valley of the Lea on the east, and with a slighter fall to the north where the tributaries of the Walbrook created a marshy area which was to become greatly enlarged in medieval times, as a result of the deterioration of the land drainage system. Since the Neolithic age the land surface of the lower Thames valley, and, indeed, all southern England, has become submerged to an approximate depth of 15 feet (the remains of a yew forest have been noted at Tilbury 12½ feet below Trinity High Water) so that in Roman times, assuming the process to have been continual, the river must have been more easily crossed than it is today. There is an entry in the *Anglo-Saxon Chronicle* of 1114 which strengthens this assumption: 'In this year [1114] also was so great an ebb tide everywhere in one day . . . so that men went riding and walking over the Thames eastward of London Bridge.' That was 800 years ago, and nearly the

3 Iron Age settlement at Heathrow, Middlesex ▶

4 Marble head of Mercury

same distance in time from Roman London, and not only does it help one to realise river conditions long ago, but points to one of the prime reasons for the siting of the city, which was its suitability for the building of the bridge, the vital link which made it accessible to and from south and south-west Britain.

A curious reverse process compensatory to this lowering of the ground level has, over the ages, been taking place along the river bank flanking the city, that is the wholesale dumping of earth and rubbish, and the pushing out of wharves and jetties so that the river is actually narrower by 200 feet or more than it was in Roman times. No doubt this constriction has resulted in a scouring and deepening of the channel and an increased tidal turbulence, conditions which had they been present in Roman times might have militated against the selection of the city site. In the city the accumulation of rubbish, ash and debris of all kinds, overlaying the gravel which is the natural building level, varies between 10 and 20 feet in depth.

The Walbrook has been mentioned above as the axial line of the city, and there can be little doubt, that the earliest settlement was on its eastern bank, which has been dignified by the term 'hillside'—for it here rose to a height of 30 feet above river level, whilst the western bank was even higher. The Walbrook, now hidden from sight beneath the huge commercial structures of today, and relegated to the disreputable status of 'drain', was in ancient times an important channel with a width of 14 feet. Although it was quite shallow, and is unlikely to have been navigable for any but small craft, its flood-plain was up to 300 feet in width, and the whole of this area was subject to flooding. To counteract this, dumping of clay and other materials took place. Wooden revetments held in place all this material, together with deposits of peaty clay and silt. By the middle of the second century A.D., conditions seem to have been stabilised, and by the end of the century, important structures such as the famous 'Walbrook Mithraeum' were built there. Earlier buildings were supported by piles and timber rafts. Finally, it is thought, the revetments collapsed through neglect and, perhaps, the gradual rising of the water level, which was taking place in southern England, contributed to the renewal of flooding.

The sources of the Walbrook were a number of small streams rising to the

orth of Hoxton and Shoreditch. Four of these streams passed under the
ity wall in the Moorfields area through brick-lined culverts, uniting into a
ngle stream which flowed across the site of what is now the Bank of
ngland, where it was joined by more tributaries flowing from inside the
ity from the north-west. When the culverts became choked, the city wall
nust have become an obstruction in the nature of a dam, holding back the
vater and converting Moorfields into something more like marsh fields.

Southwark, the south end of London Bridge, lies outside the city now as
n the past, and in Roman times it seems only to have been a suburb, a straggle
of buildings along the road from the south, which was probably lined with
ombs in the Roman fashion. It has been suggested that the south bank may
ave been the centre for entertainments, presumably because of the well-
nown tendency for like to follow like (temple then church, for instance).
Unfortunately no evidence has come to light to support this idea. To suggest
hat the comedies of Plautus should have been enacted at Southwark, to be
ollowed at an interval of 1400 years by the comedies of William Shakes-
peare, is perhaps too obvious an attempt to bridge the ages.

Londinium, lying on the north bank, was in truth, the bridge-head to
Britain, and if the historian could show the advance of the legions from the
outh, the building of the bridge and then the development of the city as an
mbattled camp or fortress, the springboard for a series of campaigns to the
north and west, then London would be shown to have a dramatic and secure
nilitary origin—nothing could be more out of character and tradition than
his! It is unlikely that events moved in that clockwork methodical way, for
is a trading and administrative centre it began, and probably will end. Some
uthorities would have it that Caesar in 54 B.C. bridged the Thames at
London, though nobody can seriously believe that this bridge would be
arefully maintained by the Britons for nearly a hundred years in readiness
or the Roman conquest which must have seemed inevitable sooner or later.
A temporary floating bridge is a possibility, but it is more likely that Caesar
used fords upstream.

As Roman London cannot be considered as an isolated fact in history,
but rather as something formed by events, as well as a causative entity, some
account of the conquest and subsequent history of Roman Britain is necessary.

5 *Silver box and strainer, from the Mithraeum*

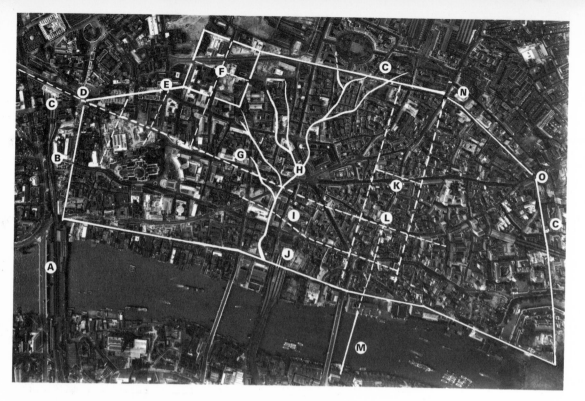

6 *Plan of Roman London superimposed on a recent aerial photograph. The white lines indicate the defensive walls, including the disputed river-wall. The broken lines indicate what has been discovered, or cautiously deduced, of the street plan.*

A	Blackfriars Barge	I	Mithraeum
B	Ludgate	J	Governor's Palace
C	Cemeteries	K	Basilica
D	Newgate	L	Forum
E	Aldersgate	M	Bridge
F	Fort	N	Bishopsgate
G	Baths in Cheapside	O	Aldgate
H	Walbrook		

7 *Roman London in about A.D. 50* ▶

8 *Silver figure of Harpocrates*

Caesar's conquest of Gaul, extending to Brittany and the Channel coast, meant that considerable numbers of fugitives fled to join their already established Belgic kinsmen in southern Britain who had already given succour to their cause. Caesar decided to secure his northern flank and, at the same time, intimidate the islanders with a demonstration of the power of Rome. He accomplished all this in two successive invasions in 55 and 54 B.C. He penetrated to the north of the Thames and captured Cassivellaunus' *oppidum* at Wheathamstead. Cassivellaunus, the overlord of south-east Britain, surrendered and accepted Roman protection, hostages were given and tribute was promised. Then Caesar sailed away—gladly, one might think—after his experience of high tides which damaged his ships, and British chariot tactics which disconcerted his troops. He is thought to have crossed the Thames near Brentford, and there are no grounds to support the legend that he built a bridge at London.

Caesar's expeditions achieved little in a military sense, and the tribute payments soon lapsed, but to use the contemporary idiom he had 'put Britain on the map', and thereafter annexation sooner or later became a certainty. Meanwhile, Roman traders brought the luxuries of the Roman world to the chiefs and kinglets in exchange for cattle and hides, gold and slaves. This is the period when a pre-Roman Londinium could have come into being but, in fact, Camulodunum—the modern Colchester—seems to have had the distinction of being the first commercial port of Britain. As the capital of the Belgic overlord Cunobelinus it was the seat of political power. Consequently, when the long-expected Roman invasion came in A.D. 43 (British princely exiles and foolish claims for their extradition were sufficient excuse for it), there can be no doubt that the British aristocracy, who were the fighting men, were well acquainted with the material advantages of Roman rule, and possibly this may in some degree have accounted for the initial rapid success of Claudius's campaign.

Four legions, that is, 25,000 men, with strong forces of auxiliaries, landed on the coast of Kent, and Richborough became the great base-camp. The Britons, who had been misled by reports of mutiny by the legionaries, had no force ready to oppose the landing, but later they rallied, and there was a pitched battle when the advancing Romans forced the passage of the Medway. The Britons fell back on the Thames, but were cut off by the Romans. Cassius Dio, who wrote about A.D. 150–235 describes this operation: 'Thence the Britons retired to the River Thames at a point where it empties into the ocean and at flood-tide forms a lake. This they easily crossed because they knew where the firm ground and the easy passages in this region were to be found; but the Romans in attempting to follow them were not so successful. However, the German auxiliaries swam across again and some others got over by a bridge a little way upstream, after which they assailed the barbarians from several sides at once and cut down many of them. In pursuing the remainder incautiously, they got into swamps from which it was difficult to make their way out, and so lost a number of men.' This extract is obviously of great value and interest. Unfortunately if one accepts it completely the reference to 'a bridge a little way upstream' seems to cancel out the claim that 'the firm ground and the easy passages' refer to the hard gravel banks of Roman London, for it is at this point precisely, 'where the river empties into the ocean and at flood-tide forms a lake'—we call it now the Pool of London—that London Bridge was afterwards built because *there* was the hard gravel which formed a uniquely suitable foundation. Where then could Dio's bridge have stood, 'a little way upstream'? There may have been an ancient track and crossing at Westminster, and historians suggest that the bridge may have been a temporary structure flung across the river by the engineers to assist the advancing troops. Conceivably this British trackway and the military bridge were connected. But perhaps the dissection of a tale, probably passed on by word of mouth and recorded by Dio at least 100 years after the events he recorded, can be carried to extremes, and it is better to extract what we can and leave the rest in its obscurity. Even so, how satisfying it would be if we could, for instance, positively identify the 'swamps' as the little valley of the Walbrook.

Securely in possession of the river crossing, the Roman commander-in-chief, Aulus Plautius, now paused to build up his supplies, organise his communications, and await the arrival of the Emperor Claudius who would lead his legions to Camulodunum, the centre of British resistance, and achieve what he craved for, the glory of a triumph. This pause at the Thames

9 *The Emperor Claudius*

17

10 *Porphyry funeral urn*

was for 40 days, and it may well be that in this interval the first London Bridge was constructed, though probably this was only a temporary military structure or a bridge of boats, such as we see recorded on Trajan's Column. Clearly this structure was the first of many bridges on the site, for during the 400 years of Roman occupation natural decay must have destroyed the bridges at more or less regular intervals, quite apart from the toll of fire and war. It would seem that no attempt was made to build a stone bridge until very much later, in medieval times.

The invasion of Claudius was entirely different in its intention and strategy from Caesar's punitive expeditions. Annexation of the whole land was now the objective, and from Richborough through London the legions fanned out northward and westward. Claudius duly entered Camulodunum and received the submission of 11 kings, all in 16 days. Then he returned to Rome, and the extension and consolidation of the conquest was left in professional hands. No doubt there was great relief when this stuttering, limping, able and clever man left Britain. Later he was to name his ill-fated son Britannicus.

That road building followed the march of the legions can be taken as axiomatic. From Richborough and the coast they converged to unite at Canterbury and drove on to Rochester, Crayford and London. This was the way of the legions. Later roads begin at Hastings, Pevensey and Chichester, and there are two other roughly parallel roads going almost due north from the Sussex coast, and linking up with the before-mentioned roads to London. All these lead to London Bridge. North of the river four more 'legionary roads', for such they were, went north-east to Chelmsford and Colchester, north to Lincoln, north-west to St Albans, and west to Silchester. Londinium was the centre of the organism that gave out and drew into itself the life and energy of the land, and so, with a doubtful interval in Saxon times, it has remained ever since.

In the beginning Londinium was only a convenient bridge-head transit camp—never a fortress—and the Imperial Cult was established at Camulodunum in a great new Temple of Claudius. A Senate House and a theatre were built, and a colony of veterans was instituted: it was the administrative capital of the province. Boudicca destroyed Camulodunum in A.D. 60 and, although

11 *Roman wells to the west of Walbrook. 21 have been found; some of them, no doubt when they silted up, were used as rubbish dumps and have yielded diverse objects to modern excavators (see plate 29)*

12 Funeral urn containing ashes, c. A.D. 100

it was rebuilt, nothing could prevent the gradual transference of the government to Londinium. Eventually the provincial treasury and the civil government were established there; after A.D. 100 it was garrisoned like a provincial capital, and Londinium was supreme. In size the city, with its area of 325 acres within the walls, far surpassed all other Romano-British towns, and was only approached by Cirencester, St Albans and Wroxeter with their approximately 200 acres.

Southern and eastern Britain and the midlands came rapidly under Roman domination, domination thinly disguised as 'alliance' in many parts of the country. But Caractacus, the implacable opponent of the invaders, was not captured until A.D. 51 and there was intermittent warfare on the Welsh and northern frontiers, with, one might suppose, the assumption that the Romans would, before long, again leap forward. Against this background of frontier warfare, and greatly increased though still conditional security, can be set the incoming tide of the imperial power bringing with it not only a great increase in the contagious habits of luxury, but the capacity to satisfy them, the dispersal and redistribution of wealth, the desire of the subject kinglets and nobles to vie in splendour with the newcomers —for these reasons, and most importantly because of its unrivalled geographical position, Londinium grew rapidly. Even in these early years it is difficult to think of it in other terms than as a great cosmopolitan trading mart, open now to cargoes from the Rhine, the Gallic ports, Spain and the Mediterranean. Inland, at last, traders could travel safely along good roads to all parts of the occupied territory. No doubt barter was the usual form of transaction, but the native British had a considerable coinage of gold and silver (and in Essex bronze too) in pre-conquest times, though this was gradually ousted by the imported Roman coins. This was inevitable because after the conquest the British mints were not allowed to continue their function. A high proportion of this importation of coin must have been channeled through Londinium, and it needs no great imagination to realise that much wealth in this way not only came to the city but must also have remained in it.

The history of Londinium lies in its stones and fragmentary remains of building plans, and in the tell-tale stratification of the black ash which means fire, and rubble and natural clay, and gravel, and the multitude of objects of all kinds which have been found imbedded therein. Small areas of metalled road surface have been linked on the city plan so that a ghostly road network has been tentatively established, and black silt, which when cut through, describes exactly the shape of the defensive ditch which it clogged. From such indications the true history of Londinium has become known to us.

Of written contemporary records there remains very little. Sir Mortimer Wheeler in his Royal Commission Inventory of 1928, which is the foundation of all our knowledge of Roman Londinium, lists two classical historians, Tacitus (about A.D. 55–120) and Ammianus Marcellinus, who wrote of events which happened in their own day. Cassius Dio (about A.D. 150–236), who has been quoted above, wrote long after the events he describes and is 'vague and unsatisfactory'. Eumenius (about A.D. 260–311), the private secretary to Constantinus Chlorus, wrote a fulsome and apparently inaccurate account of the campaign against the usurper Allectus, but lets a pinpoint of light illumine a Londinium desperately beset, a brief passing glimpse of the decaying state. Ptolemy the geographer (about A.D. 100–151) mentions Londinium with Richborough and Canterbury as principal cities of Kent, a grouping which to us would seem to be eccentric. The Antonine Itinerary of the early third century emphasises the importance of Londinium as the focal point of the road system of the province, naming it no less than seven times, from London to Dover, from London to York, and so on. It is recorded that a Bishop of London attended the Council of Arles in A.D. 314, and the Notitia Dignitatum, variously dated between 300–428, mentions 'officer in charge of the Treasury at Augusta [London]', an indication of the financial importance of the city at that late date. A Bishop of London is named in a martyrology of the sixth century, when the city was known as 'Augusta', a title of honour which was conferred on it in the fourth century, and finally there are two Byzantine references to 'Lindonion' and 'Londinium Augusti'. No further written references to Londinium occur until the medieval chroniclers began to weave their fabulous legends, some of which may be far off, distorted echoes of real historical happenings. Geoffrey of Monmouth (1100–1154) must have first place amongst these romancers, then Geraldus Cambrensis (1146–1220). Jocelyn, a monk of

13 *A figure, perhaps a rustic god, from the Mithraeum*

14 *Bronze jug, first century A.D.*

Furness (about 1200), and Fitzstephen (about 1200) had their feet more firmly on the ground, and with John Stow (1525–1605) we come to the first generation of the modern scientific recorders of Roman remains.

In the 17 years following the conquest, Londinium, which by the evidence of first-century pottery discovered on the eastern bank of the Walbrook had its nucleus in that locality, grew into what Tacitus describes as 'a place not indeed distinguished by the title of "colony", but crowded with traders, and a great centre of commerce'—a foretaste of modern London where commerce rather than formal grandeur or amenity is the rule. There were, significantly, no defences. The legions had pressed on to the frontiers, where the governor, Suetonius Paulinus, was striking at the stronghold of Druidism in Anglesey. This shrewdly conceived campaign aimed at the roots of British resistance was completely successful, but Suetonius was frustrated in his further objective—the subjugation of the still resisting tribes—by a sudden and unexpected rebellion in the south-east.

Boudicca, widow of King Prasutagus of the Iceni, was scourged, and her daughters insulted and outraged by the cruel and stupid officials who were proceeding to incorporate the wealth and lands of the Iceni into the province, and treating the natives as newly conquered vassals. The Iceni were joined in their revolt by the neighbouring Trinovantes, who had their own reasons for discontent. The huge British army moved against the unwalled Camulodunum, sacked it and butchered the population with ghastly cruelty. The ninth legion rashly challenged the victors and was nearly wiped out. Suetonius hurried back to London with a cavalry force, leaving the legions to follow. But he could not hold London (or St Albans) and the citizens were faced with the agonising choice of either remaining in the defenceless city, or abandoning their shops and houses and possessions and following the troops to their point of concentration in the west.

Those who trusted to the mercy of the Iceni were slaughtered. London was consumed by fire and ringed with the crucified victims of Boudicca's vengeance. There were 80,000 of these victims, though we are uncertain how many of them were involved in the sack of London. The mark of the disaster remains to this day in a layer of burnt red ash, fragments of Samian ware, coins of Claudius fused by fire, wattle and daub mingled with wall plaster, all found at a depth of between 10 and 13 feet and resting on the original gravel, in the area between Gracechurch Street and Walbrook.

A great number of human skulls have been found in modern times in the stream-bed of the Walbrook, and there is in Geoffrey of Monmouth's *Historia Britonum* a curious reference to a mass execution on the banks of a brook which has been identified as the Walbrook. The romancer dates this execution to the capture of the city from the supporters of the usurper Allectus in A.D. 296, but it is conceivable that Boudicca, and not the Roman general Asclepiodotus was responsible for the massacre, and that Geoffrey of Monmouth had heard, but wrongly interpreted, one of those faint whispers from the past, which have been mentioned above.

The inevitable Roman counterblow resulted in the death of Boudicca with a vast slaughter of the vanquished Britons. Suetonius initiated a policy of ruthless repression and vindictive revenge, but Julius Classicianus, the newly appointed Procurator, the Chief Treasury Official who could report direct to the Emperor, appealed against this policy (either on humanitarian grounds or because of the bad effects on the economy of the Province) and pacification was thereafter effected by milder measures. It is indicative of the importance of London—which must have rapidly recovered from its destruction—that the tomb of Classicianus, who died in office, has been discovered in London, and not in Camulodunum, which was still presumably the official provincial capital. The upper part of the inscription stone, with the decorative surmounting scrolls almost intact, was found in 1852. It had been reused as building material in the bastion of the city wall at Trinity Place north of the Tower. One can suppose it was treated in this disrespectful way long after the time of Classicianus, and in a moment of emergency, when it was necessary to construct a defensive work with any material that came to hand. Then in 1935 the lower part of the inscription was found, including the abbreviated title 'Proc. Provinc. Brit.'

Although there is no written history of Londinium, between A.D. 61 and 296 there is evidence that the city which grew up after the Boudicca destruction possessed a far greater degree of splendour, and an altogether larger scale than its Claudian predecessor. Whilst the Claudian city had buildings of stone as well as timber and daub, they were probably the exception rather

15 Marble figure of a river god, second century A.D.

23

16 Roman London in about A.D. 100 ▶

17 *Roman well with square oak frame, on the site of the Bank of London and South America, Queen Street*

than not, but in the later city stonebuilt structures became more frequent. A Basilica 500 feet long was built, a great Governor's Palace arose, and a fragment of a temple inscription has been discovered which from its scale suggests an important building.

Prosperity is likely to have been proportionate to this architectural development, and the construction of what we know as the 'Cripplegate Fort' in the early years of the second century seems to shew that military requirements whether administrative or ceremonial were of great importance in this essentially commercial city. But the construction of this important fortification in a secure part of the province in a time of peace must always remain something of a mystery.

The prosperity of Londinium in these years met with one serious disaster, the great fire of the time of Hadrian, between 125 and 130, which has left a layer of ash spread over 65 acres, in itself an indication of the city's growth since A.D. 61. It also shews that much of the building then destroyed may have been closely packed, and still of timber construction.

The popular idea of a city of classical times as being brightly coloured and checker-board planned, with colonnaded temples and public buildings occurring at regular intervals and everything very tidy and clean, has probably never been true of any city of any period. Londinium, whilst it had some regularity in its street plan, and large public buildings, must also have had the familiar mixture of splendour and squalor, and a casual sprinkling of commercial buildings of all kinds, of stone, brick, timber, wattle and daub, tile and thatch. Fine metalled roads with stone curbs on either side, and muddy lanes with open drains running down the centre. Cess pits were used and the Walbrook with its tributaries and the river served, as they still did in modern times, as open sewers.

Some areas within the walls were scarcely built upon—the Romans in Britain always had a tendency to include in their walled towns far more land than could ever be occupied. In fact, the over ambitious scale of their towns points to the failure of the attempt to install in Britain a Mediterranean type of Romanization or urbanization.

It has been suggested that the city wall was built towards the end of the second century, and the fact that it was built at that period can indeed be related to the internal stresses of the Empire rather than to the threat of foreign enemies. When Commodus was murdered in A.D. 192 there ensued a period of anarchic civil war. Clodius Albinus, then Governor of Britain, was one of the three claimants to the Empire. The more powerful Septimius Severus placated Albinus whilst he dealt with his more serious rival Pescennius Niger, but after his victory over the latter two years later declared Albinus a public enemy. Albinus not to be outdone, declared himself emperor and invaded Gaul but was defeated and killed. The campaigns of Severus were made necessary by the disruption which resulted from Albinus' withdrawal of the troops guarding Hadrian's Wall. The wild Picts took advantage of this to raid into Britain, and Severus found it necessary not only to chastise them but to reorganise entirely the defences of the province. It might be said that in the last years of the second century Roman Britain faltered, and that never again was there to be the forward thrusting self-confidence which up to that time had characterised the régime. Albinus was already Governor of Britain in 192, and not until 197 was he defeated and killed in Gaul. He must have known that a conflict between him and either Niger or Severus was inevitable, and the idea has been put forward that it was in the knowledge of this inescapable future that Albinus ordered the building of city walls, not only at London, but all over the province. That cities should have defensive walls had been continental practice from time immemorial, and Albinus may have been merely conforming to this familiar convention of 'walled towns'—and conformity was dear to the Roman heart—but the expenditure of treasure and labour and material must have been prodigious, and one seeks a special reason for this transformation from a peace to a war footing.

The five years' grace enjoyed by Albinus gave him ample time to complete these works. One may compare the seven years in which Hadrian's engineers built the vast northern defence system that bears his name, and the mere 40 days in which, we are told, the enormous land walls of Constantinople were re-erected after a disastrous earthquake—although anyone who has seen the remains of the latter must feel a degree of scepticism about that supposed achievement.

Not until much later was there to be fear of the foreign foe in southern

18 Inscribed tile, from Warwick Lane, Newgate Street

19 Sculptures (hand of Mithras, Serapis, Mercury) found in the Mithraeum

Britain, and therefore, if defences were built at that time, they were against enemies within the empire, i.e. Septimius Severus. It can, of course, be argued that the realistic commander in Britain would appreciate that his cause would have reached the point of defeat whenever a continental rival had effected a landing, that in a defensive war his defeat would be certain, and therefore the construction of defensive walls and ditches merely an extravagant waste of effort. However, the military mind is not always logical and the Maginot Line stopping short at the Belgian frontier is a modern instance of this. A 'secure base' has always been a favoured principle of war, and the arguments in favour of Albinus as the builder of London's wall are strong. Even so, archaeological opinion is far from unanimous in this dating: Sir Mortimer Wheeler, in his Royal Commission Report of 1928, expressed the view that it was built within 50 years of the Boudiccan rebellion; Haverfield tentatively named the late third century; some authorities believe it was Constantinian; others, Hadrianic. Professor Grimes in his post-war excavations discovered a worn coin of 183 in a deposit ante-dating the wall, and this with other evidence gives weight to the last years of the second century as the most likely building date.

Severus divided Britain into two provinces, Upper and Lower Britain. York became the capital of lower Britain, and London, almost certainly, of upper Britain. Severus, by this division of authority was guarding against a too powerful governor of a united Britain again rebelling against the central authority of Rome. It is interesting to note, however, that this did not prevent the rebellion of Carausius and Allectus, or the proclamation of Constantine as Emperor at York.

We do not know whether this reduction in status had any effect on Londinium's prosperity, but when Severus died at York in 211, there began a long period of chaos, with puppet emperors succeeding each other at short intervals, with assassination as the normal culmination of a reign. With the barbarians pressing everywhere more strongly upon the weakened defences and even endangering Rome itself, it seemed that nothing could save the Roman world from destruction. There were emperors of Gaul, independent of Rome, and from 259–274 Britain was included in this Gaulish Empire of Posthumus and his successors. Finally in 284 Diocletian came to power, and achieved a miracle of reorganisation and reconstruction, though at heavy cost in personal liberty, and only by putting such a weight of taxation and a multiplication of authority upon the shoulders of the people that poverty and distress became endemic all over the Empire.

Londinium, largely dependent on her foreign trade, must have suffered acutely through all these years, probably more than did those towns, bearing some likeness to our 'country' towns, which subsisted on, and were surrounded by, a self-contained rural economy. Londinium was on the downgrade, though important houses decorated with fine mosaics were still being erected within the walls. Probably Britain suffered less from the tumultuous times than did the ravaged continental provinces, but towards the end of the third century a new and serious menace appeared, when Saxon pirates began to raid the southern and eastern shores of Britain. The Romans were prompt in their counter measures: a system of signal-towers to warn the fleet of the raiders' approach, sea patrols of fast green-painted galleys, the general policy at this time being one of interception at sea rather than static coastal defence works. Carausius, a Belgian of great strength and ability, was appointed Admiral of the Channel Fleet, the Classis Britannica, but soon charges were brought against him that he was inclined to intercept the raiders on their return voyage loaded with loot, which he then shared with them. Forestalling the sentence of death pronounced by Maximian (co-Emperor with Diocletian) Carausius revolted, had himself proclaimed Emperor, and for six years ruled Britain and the Low Countries, defied all efforts to subdue him, and even finally wrested some sort of recognition from the legitimate sovereigns. Carausius minted coins in London and appears to have been an efficient and popular ruler.

He was murdered by Allectus, his chief finance minister, in 294. In 296, Constantius Chlorus besieged and captured Boulogne, the base of the Classis Britannica, and then invaded Britain. The campaign is described by Eumenius in a panegyric of Constantius of such an exceptionally servile nature that the reader instinctively distrusts his account and with a certain justification, since it is only with the help of the summaries left by Aurelius Victor, Eutropius and Orosius, all of a later date, that a balanced viewpoint can be attained. But one very important point is established, that in those days he who held London held Britain.

Constantius divided his armada into two forces; one under his personal

20 Iron Age boar, from Hounslow

21 *Key to plate 22*

A	Aldgate	J	Fort
B	Stane Street	K	Baths in Cheapside
C	Bishopsgate	L	Site of St Paul's Cathedral
D	Basilica and Forum	M	Pottery kilns
E	Governor's Palace	N	Aldersgate
F	Walbrook	O	Newgate
G	Mithraeum	P	Ludgate
H	Cemeteries	Q	Blackfriars Barge
I	Cripplegate		

22 *Roman London in the third century A.D.* ▶

Alan Sorrell 1961

23 *Iron sword with bronze scabbard*

command sailed round the North Foreland, whilst the other, under the command of the Prefect Asclepiodotus, avoiding the fleet of Allectus 'watching in ambush by the Isle of Wight', in dense fog landed an army on the coast of Hampshire. Allectus apparently had posted his army near London to oppose the expected onslaught of Constantius, who seems to have been remarkably slow in his movements, perhaps confused by the same fog that had aided Asclepiodotus. Abandoning his prepared position, Allectus rushed to oppose the Hampshire landing, but was defeated and killed in battle. Survivors of his decimated army retreated towards London—Eumenius describes them as 'barbarian mercenaries'—and they began to plunder the city. Fortunately at that very moment the fleet of Constantius emerged from the fog, and discovered that it was sailing up the Thames. Constantius put troops ashore, attacked the barbarian mercenaries and 'slew them in the streets'.

Eumenius claims that this induced a 'sentiment of pleasure and gratitude' in the citizens, but he does not describe the feelings of Asclepiodotus at having the laurels so neatly plucked from his brow by Constantius. Perhaps the 'pleasure and gratitude' were related not so much to the killing of their former defenders, but to relief at the end of the period of semi-isolation, and to the hope of the resumption of regular trade with the Empire, which surely must have been seriously interrupted as a result of the policies of Carausius and Allectus. The happy event was commemorated by the striking of a handsome gold medallion showing on its reverse, Constantius on horseback with a galley below, and a kneeling figure and gate-towers symbolising the city. LON is an abbreviation of Londinium, and the inscription reads REDDITOR LUCIS AETERNAE, 'the restorer of the eternal light'. If the medallion had been minted in London it might have been claimed that the gate-towers had some degree of portrait accuracy, but since it was minted in Trier it is unlikely that this is so.

Constantius remained in Britain and made York, not London, his headquarters. This indicates that his prime attention was given to the military needs of rebuilding in the north, and the re-establishing of the Wall which had been stripped of its garrison by Allectus, with a Pictish raid as its inevitable consequence. The damage had been very serious, and Chester as well as York had been devastated. With indomitable courage and resolution all this was repaired. Constantius rebuilt York in splendid fashion and established a chain of great forts along the east and south coasts. Known to us as Saxon shore forts, their purpose was to provide bases for land and sea forces to combat the increasing menace of Saxon raiders. Constantius even mounted a retributive campaign beyond the northern frontier. The concentrations of authority in York must have depressed London's political importance, though it is unlikely to have interfered with its supremacy as a trading centre. Sir Mortimer Wheeler aptly refers to London as the 'nerve centre of the province' and compares the transient strategical primacy of York with the permanence of London's unrivalled key position, but the drastic reorganisation which followed Constantius' re-conquest meant that London now became merely the capital of Flavia Caesariensis, one of the four provinces into which Upper and Lower Britain had been divided. Britain became a diocese (12 in the Empire) ruled by a 'vicarius'. But London remained the 'nerve centre', the great city, whatever political demotion she may have suffered. London's lack of formal status was quite remarkable; she was neither municipality nor colony nor civitas—that is cantonal capital. This aloofness is peculiar, particularly when there is reason to think that it was the residence of the Procurator, the chief financial officer of the administration.

The whole problem bristles with contradictions—the acknowledged premier city of the land, but with the official status of a small provincial capital, on a level with Cirencester. Not until William the Conqueror became King in 1066 did London become the undisputed capital and, even then, the purist might claim that Westminster, and not the city, became the administrative centre. So has it remained to this day, the city intent on its commercial life, aloof from government and all else that might interfere with that first reason for its existence.

Constantius died in 306, and Constantine, later called the Great, was proclaimed at York by his soldiers, quite illegally, as emperor in succession to his father. The reorganisation of Diocletian had divided the Empire into East and West, with five junior emperors entitled Caesar. Constantius at his

24 Bronze legionary helmet, first century A.D., showing plume-holder and attachment for cheek-piece

25 *Cult slab from the Mithraeum showing Mithras slaying a bull, second century A.D.*

death was co-emperor, and Constantine was then allowed the rank of Caesar by Galerius the surviving Emperor. Subsequently he became sole Emperor, embraced the Christian faith, more perhaps from reasons of policy than conviction, and died in 337 after the longest reign since Augustus.

London has never been famed as a religious centre, and the remains of temples and churches of the Roman period are few. As has been noted above, a bishop of London, Restitutus, with two other British bishops, attended the council held at Arles in 314, the year following the Edict of Milan which formally recognised Christianity. So we may assume the existence of a church in London at that date, though nothing has survived to indicate its site or architectural character. The rival sect of Mithraism, archaeologically speaking, has survived in a more impressive way in the famous Walbrook Mithraeum, discovered by Professor Grimes in 1954. Other Mithraic sculpture has been found in Drury Lane. London, from its position as the chief entry port of Britain, must have always had a markedly cosmopolitan population and this accounts for the spread of foreign religious beliefs of all denominations, and may have served Christianity as in earlier days it had served the Roman military machine—as a funnel through which the country was fertilised and subdued.

The age of Constantine seems to have been a period of revived prosperity in Britain, and a strong centralised imperial government no doubt provided a good climate for overseas trade, from which London must have benefited.

But beyond the frontiers the menace of Picts, Scots and Saxons remained ever present, and in 342 Constans visited Britain and quietened the Picts and Scots by making concessions—an ominous precedent—after a destructive raid in which Corbridge was probably burnt; this means that the defences of Hadrian's Wall had been pierced. Then in 350 Magnentius, a native-born Briton, revolted, slew Constans, and for a time ruled Britain and all the west including Rome itself. But he was overthrown in 353. Julian, nephew of the great Constantine, was appointed Caesar of the Gallic provinces and sent his general Lupicinus to Britain in 360 to deal with the continuing serious inroads of the Picts. Lupicinus made London his headquarters, so it is clear that no downgrading of the city's official status could deny its rightful place as the effective capital of the British provinces. On the

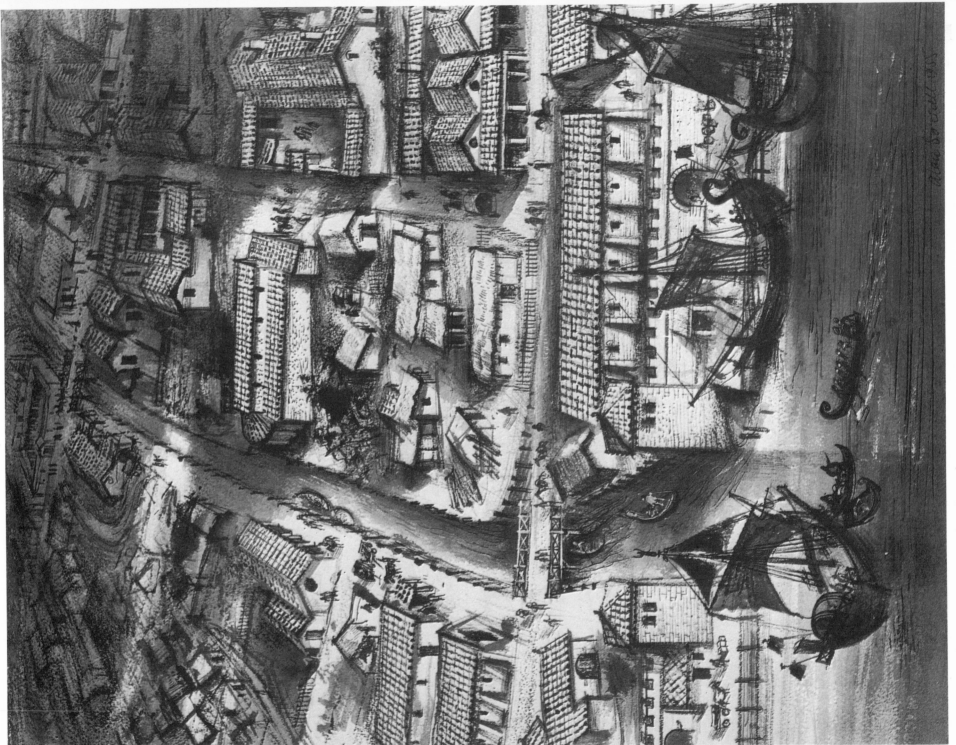

26 *The Walbrook, with the Mithraeum, from the south*

27 *Figure of Roman soldier*

other hand, if London was the base for a campaign it suggests that barbarian penetration may have reached far beyond the frontier regions.

Then in 367 there occurred a disaster which finally wrecked the hitherto prosperous villa economy of Britain and devastated the countryside. This great raid was made by the Picts, Scots and Saxons, a combination so unlikely that it was outside Roman military planning. The barbarian tidal wave spread over the whole land, only the walled towns standing like rocks above the flood. The invaders, whose only thought was destruction and plunder, split into small bands which roved the countryside burning and destroying and murdering those unfortunate people who could not or would not seek refuge in the towns. So that when Valentinian's general, Count Theodosius, landed at Sandwich with his veteran legions he was not opposed by any concentration of force. He marched to London, defeating on his way several small parties of the barbarians, releasing multitudes of captives and retrieving much spoil, a small proportion of which he distributed amongst his troops.

The citizens of London, who had almost despaired of succour, joyfully opened their gates to Theodosius, and the city became his headquarters. In the ensuing campaign detachments of the imperial troops sought out, ambushed and destroyed the invaders until once more the land was freed. The ravages were repaired and the Wall re-established, but the prosperity of the country was irretrievably shattered, never to return in Roman times.

London must have played an important and honourable part in the reconquest, for it received the title of 'Augusta' at this time. Ammianus writes of 'Augusta which the ancients used to call Lundinium', but the new honorific, except for official use, did not long survive. Only 15 years after the great disaster of 367 Magnus Maximus had himself proclaimed Emperor of Britain, stripped the defences of their garrisons and invaded the continent. After a time he was defeated, by Theodosius, the son of his old commander Count Theodosius. Yet again the barbarians overran the weakly-held British defences. This deplorably monotonous repeating pattern of events ruined Roman Britain and, with it, London. The countryside being no longer safe may well have meant that the walled cities became crowded with refugees with all the attendant congestion, disruption and disease. There cannot have been very much import and export trade, and London can be imagined as ruinous and decayed, with a starving population—for the devastated countryside would have meant that corn, the British staple, must have been in short supply, certainly with no grain available for export. Curious enough is the fact that the coinage retained a relatively high standard of design and content. Maximus issued a fine gold solidus from the revived London mint, which after his downfall seems to have come to an end. It is surprising to come upon this fine coin of 380–388 of such a superior quality when compared with the miserably barbarous coins of the third century when the economy was undoubtedly in a far more prosperous state.

The Romans were possessed of a capacity for resilience which assumes the character of heroism in these shadowy anguished final years of Roman Britain. Thus, Stilicho came to Britain in 395, and once more reorganised its defences. One can imagine a partial recovery, but when in 407 yet another adventurer known to us as Constantine III seized control and again took an army to the continent, there could be no long survival of the old order. The famous rescript of the Emperor Honorius in 410 in which the Britons are told to look to their own defences is popularly regarded as the end of the period, but it should not be thought that there was any clear-cut end to the régime, as, for instance, of Belgian rule in the Congo. As late as 457, according to the *Anglo-Saxon Chronicle*, London gave refuge to fugitives fleeing from Saxons victorious at Crayford in Kent—though it must be added that there is a weakness in this evidence in that the account belongs to the ninth century. The Notitia Dignitatum gives no hint of disruption of authority. St Germanus visited Britain twice, in 429 and 447, and mentions wealthy magnates, a man of tribunician rank, and municipal government in the south-eastern part of Britain, which would certainly include London. Wheeler writes that the evidence is 'just strong enough to suggest that towns such as London and Verulam were able to maintain a real civic status something like half a century after the rupture with Rome' and that there exists no valid obstacle to the existence of an 'attenuated London throughout the fifth and sixth centuries'. Saxon invaders came, not as an army, but probably as infiltrators, seeking land to settle in a countryside which had been ravished and empty for half a century—that is since 367 or thereabouts.

28 *Marble group of Bacchus and companions (Silenus, satyr, maenad and panther) from the Mithraeum*

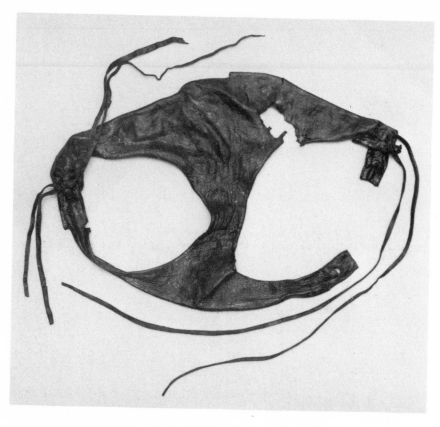

29 Leather 'bikini' trunks from first-century well (see plate 11)

Archaeological evidence shows that the Saxons made full use of the Thames route, unhampered by London or its inhabitants, and this presents some interesting thoughts relative to the river defences and the bridge. Can one visualise these hostile infiltrators passing a still rich city whose river front was unwalled, as has been argued was the case? And how was the bridge negotiated? Was it obligingly opened for them to pass through, or were their boats so small that they could creep through between the close-set timbers? The former insinuates an unbelievable cynicism or timidity, and the latter would seem to have been a physical impossibility if the bridge had been held by valorous men. The Saxons made the river passage by some means or other. The great structures in the city, the Basilica, and the Governor's Palace for instance, cannot long have survived the paralysis of neglect and disuse which now overcame them, and a picture of increasing shabbiness and decay presents itself. Rotting wharves and empty warehouses, a deserted forum, and now probably a dwindling population, diminished by emigration and disease.

But there is another side of this picture, for sculptured stones of an earlier age have been found, re-used for the fortifications, and this demonstrates not only an energetic will to live, but suggests that where so much toil was expended on the defences there must still have been much left to defend. It is now thought unlikely that London was ever abandoned and left derelict, but not until the bishopric was revived in 604 by St Augustine can it be said that London emerged from the shadows of Imperial Rome and within her ancient time-scarred walls renewed herself, now no longer Augusta Londinium, but Saxon London.

The Defences

The Roman linear defences of London are exactly defined by the later medieval city, except for a diversion between Ludgate and the river, where they were demolished by the Black Friars, with the permission of King Edward I, to give space for the enlargement of the precinct of their priory. The Roman walls were pierced by Ludgate, Newgate, Aldersgate, the north gate of the fort—which we know as Cripplegate—then Alderman-bury Postern, which in all probability was of Roman origin. Moorgate was enlarged from a medieval postern into a gateway in 1415, and was not Roman in foundation. Bishopsgate and Aldgate were both Roman, and so, it is thought, was the Tower Postern, between Aldgate and the river. The existence in Roman times of a river-wall is a vexed question and certainly no watergates have survived. All the gateways noted above, with the exception of the two posterns, served Roman roads or, as in the case of Aldersgate, earlier roads which continued in use in Roman times.

We have no positive evidence of the date of the construction of the defences but, as we have seen, the governorship of Clodius Albinus, the rival of Severus, from 192 to 197, has been suggested as the most likely date for logistic reasons—the expectation of attack by Severus—and the evidence of coins and pottery found in the internal earthbank, which is thought to have been of the same period as the wall it supported. The external projecting bastions, a reversion to a much earlier type of urban fortification, were added in the late third century. These bastions, some solid, on the east, others hollow, were on the east and west flanks of the defences, with only two bastions, with an interval of 800 yards between them, on the north. Solid bastions were an important feature of late Roman defensive works, and they were so constructed as to be suitable as mountings for heavy ballistas which could fire along the intervening lengths of wall and so take attackers in the flank. They were interdependent, and made possible successful defence with very small forces. The western group of bastions were hollow in construction, and these, it is now thought, may be of post-Roman date. No archaeological

30 *Roman and medieval city wall, Tower Hill*

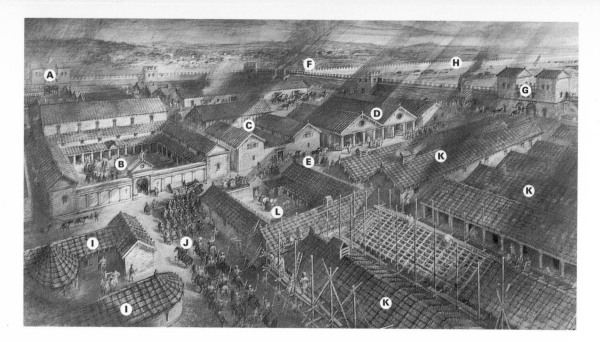

31 *Key to plate 32*

A North Gate (Cripplegate)
B Principia (headquarters)
C Praetorium (commanding officer's house and baths)
D Horrea (granaries)
E Via Principalis (Silver Street—Addle Street)

F Aldermanbury Postern
G East Gate
H City Wall
I Workshops
J Via Praetoria (Wood Street)
K Barrack blocks
L Officer's house

32 *The Fort from the south* ▶

40

Alan Sorrell 19

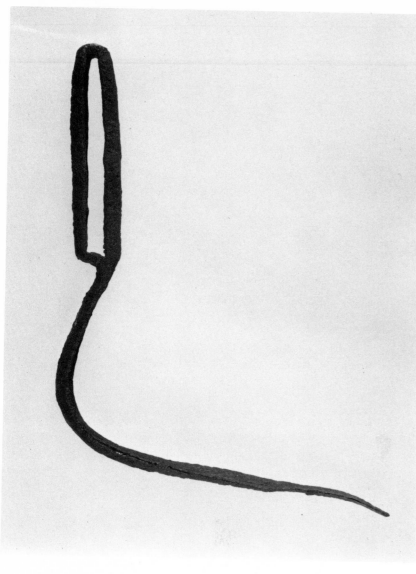

33 Iron strigil (skin-scraper)

explanation has so far been made to account for the limitation of bastions on the northern wall, other than the 'chance of non-discovery'.

The Roman wall was constructed of Kentish ragstone with a plinth of Kentish sandstone. Its core was of ragstone in its rough state set in extremely hard white mortar 'which was perhaps run into the core in a fluid state as the interstices are not completely filled' (Wheeler). This solid mass was faced externally and internally with squared and coursed ragstone blocks with an approximate measurement of nine by five inches. At three-foot vertical intervals there were triple bonding courses of Roman bricks and these were carried through the wall. Where the bonding courses occurred, the wall was reduced in thickness internally by about three inches. Thus an effect of entasis was produced which was pleasing aesthetically, although of little structural significance. Whatever were the conditions of emergency which dictated the building of the wall, they were evidently not allowed to interfere with such subtleties.

The wall stands upon a foundation of flints and puddled clay in a trench three to four feet deep cut in the natural ground. There is no absolute evidence as to the height of the wall—its highest remaining fragment recorded was about 16 feet above the plinth—but it is reasonable to suppose that to the tops of the battlements which protected the wall walk it reached a height of not less than 20 feet, whilst the thickness varied from seven to nine feet. It may be here mentioned that the height of Hadrian's Wall has been estimated as 21 feet six inches, with a mean thickness of nine feet—the latter measurement also applies to the city wall of Verulamium, and it seems likely that the dimensions of defensive walls were standardised. The usual Roman method of wall construction was to assign lengths of wall to separate gangs of workmen, and Wheeler has pointed out that this procedure is indicated in the London Wall by the faulty joining up of the bonding courses at various points. The remains of the towered gateways are scanty: only at Newgate and Aldersgate are there surviving foundations of any importance, and these demonstrate that the two gates were of a totally different form from each other. In a separate category are the remains of the west gate of the fort, and these will be referred to later.

At Bishopsgate what may have been the wall of a gatehouse projecting about 20 feet inside the wall has been found. The Newgate remains are of a simple rectangular structure measuring 95 feet by 32 feet with double gate passages. Like Aldersgate, Newgate was set awkwardly at an angle to the wall so that whilst its northern end projected seven feet beyond it, its southern end stood out fully 14 feet. It would have been normal for the ditch to have been spanned by a timber bridge wide enough to allow unimpeded access to the two gate passages—one for inward and the other for outward traffic. Aldersgate bore some resemblance to the east and west gates of Verulamium. Its sharply projecting rounded gate towers indicate a later date than Newgate's simple rectangle. Aldersgate was related to the wall even more awkwardly than Newgate and it was clearly inserted into the defences when they were already in existence. The Roman ditch has largely been destroyed by the digging of the much wider medieval one. It was v-shaped in section and varied in width from 10 to 16 feet along the greater part of its length, except at the site of the General Post Office where it had been widened in Roman times to 25 feet and deepened from the normal six and a half feet to 14.

On general grounds of military expediency there is every reason to think that a river wall existed in Roman times. It is difficult to imagine that competent military engineers would have left the city wide open to attack along its vulnerable river flank, but today archaeological opinion is cautiously opposed to the idea of a continuous defensive river wall. It should be noted that Wheeler in his 1928 report had no such doubts. There are, in fact at various points along the river frontage substantial remains of Roman walls, and it has been observed that because of the instability of the river bank special constructional methods were used, including massive timber reinforcements designed to resist the tendency of the heavy structure to slide or topple into the soft mud of the river bank. Wheeler, quoting *Archaeologia*, LXIII, records the structure of this supposed river wall in some detail: 'Large roughly squared timbers, 12 feet long and about 8 inches square, were first laid on the top of the ballast across the thickness of the wall, these being in position by pointed piles driven in at intervals . . . on these timbers were laid large irregular sandstones and ragstones bedded in clay and flints . . . above which was a bond of two rows of yellow tiles . . . chalk and other stone formed the core, the whole being cemented with red mortar.'

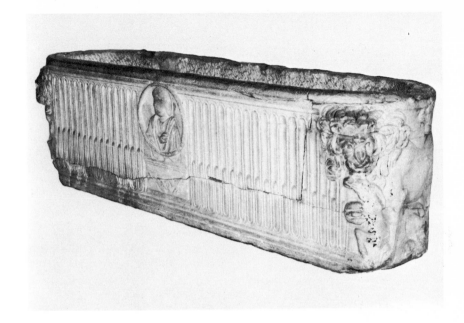

34 *Stone sarcophagus. The ends are carved with a lion mauling a goat*

35 Bronze steelyard

Further to the west of the structure described above, two fragments of massive wall were examined by Roach Smith in 1839–41. They were 350 yards apart, and in exact alignment along the river frontage. In 1961, a series of great walls was discovered adjacent to one of these fragments—in the Lambeth Hill area—and it is now believed that these walls together with the Roach Smith fragment formed part of some huge platform or quay. A right-angled turn to the north (which had, in fact, been noted by Roach Smith) is thought to be proof that no continuous riverside defensive wall existed in Roman times. However, an early medieval chronicler, the twelfth-century Fitzstephen, wrote confidently that 'on the south side also the Citie was walled and towred, but the fish full river of Thames with his ebbing and flowing hath long since subverted them', and though it cannot be proved that Fitzstephen referred to Roman walls and towers the strong probability remains. It has been pointed out that the fragmentary Roman city land-wall points directly towards the Lanthorn Tower (which was in medieval times the corner tower of the Tower of London's inner curtain), and it has been suggested that the Wakefield, Bell and Middle Towers extending westward at the appropriate intervals are perhaps founded upon Roman bastions though here again current archaeological opinion is opposed to the idea. This great defensive system can be described as the abiding Roman contribution to the shape of London.

36 Newgate, looking north–east towards the Cripplegate Fort ▸

37 South-west corner of the Fort

The Fort

The curious planning of the landward wall on the north-west side, with its deep re-entrant between Cripplegate and Newgate was thus noted by Sir Mortimer Wheeler in his Royal Commission report of 1928, 'This salient represents a skirting by the wall of a quarter already definitely laid out before the wall was built.' This deduction, from the evidence then available, was just and accurate, but not until German bombing in 1940–44 had laid bare the foundations of the Cripplegate area could Professor Grimes brilliantly confirm and expand the deduction, and shew that the presence of a pre-existent fort had there dictated the line of the city defences. Excavation showed that instead of the normal construction there were two thinner walls whose total thickness equalled that of the city wall. A typical internal fort turret on a curving anglewall was discovered—and a Roman fort 280 yards from north to south and 235 yards from east to west enclosing 12 acres had come to light. Subsequently, the remains of the West Gate, of a typical Roman military type, were traced, as well as fragmentary remains of barrack buildings and the east ditch. Wood Street running north and south is almost exactly on the line of the Via Praetoria (the main streets in Roman forts, serving the four gateways were traditionally known as Via Praetoria and Via Principalis), and Cripplegate itself was found to be in the exact position of the north gate. Intersecting Wood Street at right-angles are Silver Street and Addle Street, and they perpetuate Via Principalis. The traces of barrack buildings which have been found along the eastern side of Via Praetoria are now lost in the immensely deep foundation of the New Wood Street Police Station and the idea of a chain of command beginning in Roman times and being taken up and continued today is not entirely whimsical. Indications of the perimeter road inside the fort walls have also been found, and even the post holes for the timbers supporting the bridge over the ditch at the South Gate have been identified, although later building has effectively destroyed all traces of the headquarters building and the other structures which can be looked for in definite positions in Roman forts, for these military establishments of the Empire, whether they were in Britain or Syria, Spain or North

Africa, conformed strictly to type. The evidence of pottery and coins has led expert opinion to deduce a building date between A.D. 98–117 during the principate of Trajan, and this dating, far from solving a mystery, makes it much more mysterious. For if the fort had been built at the time of the Claudian conquest in A.D. 43 it would have had a rational purpose as a base for operations, a strong point from which the region north of the Thames could be dominated. Or if it had been built immediately after Boadicea's rebellion and her sack of London in A.D. 61 it might have been reasonably regarded as a typical 'closing of the stable door after the horse had bolted', or a belated insurance against further trouble and a stiffener of the badly shaken civilian morale of that time. But in the splendid self-confidence of Trajanic days there would have been no threat to peace and security in south-east Britain, and to station 1500 men at Londinium would have seemed an absurdity to the economical Roman military mind. Was it then, a staging-post for troops on their way to the northern frontier, or an equipment store, or an administrative centre? It is unlikely that we shall ever know. The siting of the fort, too, is peculiar, away from the river with its vital bridge. Certainly the marshes to the north, east and west gave the Cripplegate Fort strength in isolation, but a fortress is built to dominate the tactical scene, not to withdraw from it. Did the fort lose its identity when it became merged with the city, or become its citadel? Again, we may never know, though archaeological opinion inclines to the former supposition.

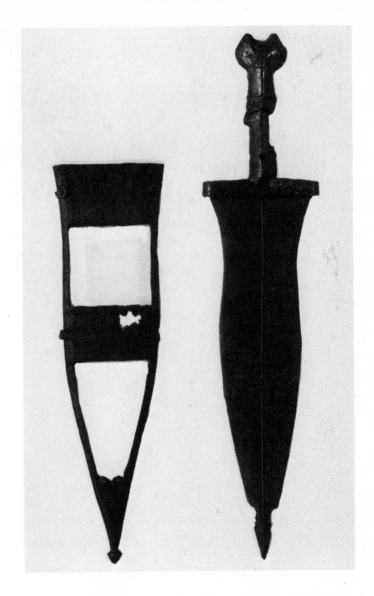

38 Iron legionary dagger and scabbard mount, first century A.D.

47

The Basilica and Forum

39 Wall and pier in the Basilica

The Basilica was the focal point of Roman London, physically as well as administratively, since it was sited so that the traveller from the south, on crossing the bridge, would have seen its great bulk immediately before and above him at the top of the hill which we now call Cornhill, and where Leadenhall Market now stands. The Basilica was 500 feet long, about the same length as St Paul's Cathedral. It was aligned east and west, parallel to the river, and must have towered above the surrounding buildings as did St Paul's before the construction of the hideously dreary office blocks which now brutally disfigure the city.

The Basilica had a total width of 150 feet, including a range of what were probably administrative offices on its north side. It was aisled. The excavated walls, however, present some confusing features: there is an unaccountable double wall extending nearly half way along the south side, and a difference in date has been detected between the various fragments which have been found in this area. It is now thought that the south aisle was open to the Forum and took the form of an open arcade. This would have meant that the Basilica, or a large portion of it, would have been in effect an extension of the Forum as a meeting place and promenade. One must suppose, however, that some portion of the Basilica would have been completely walled—it is difficult to visualise legal and administrative processes functioning in a brisk westerly gale. Archaeological opinion has now generally agreed that the Basilica was built about A.D. 80–90, and was extended westwards to its full length of 500 feet in the early second century. Evidence in the form of a thick layer of ash has been found on the site of the Basilica, which suggests that the devastating fire which occurred in the early second century may have destroyed the earlier building and so have been the reason or excuse for the extension westwards. The Romans were ever ready to satisfy their craving for glorification by splendid building, and neither disaster nor decay could prevent the expression of that lust. The Basilica summed up in one great structure all the administrative and legal functions of the state, unlike our present usage which houses law courts and government under separate roofs.

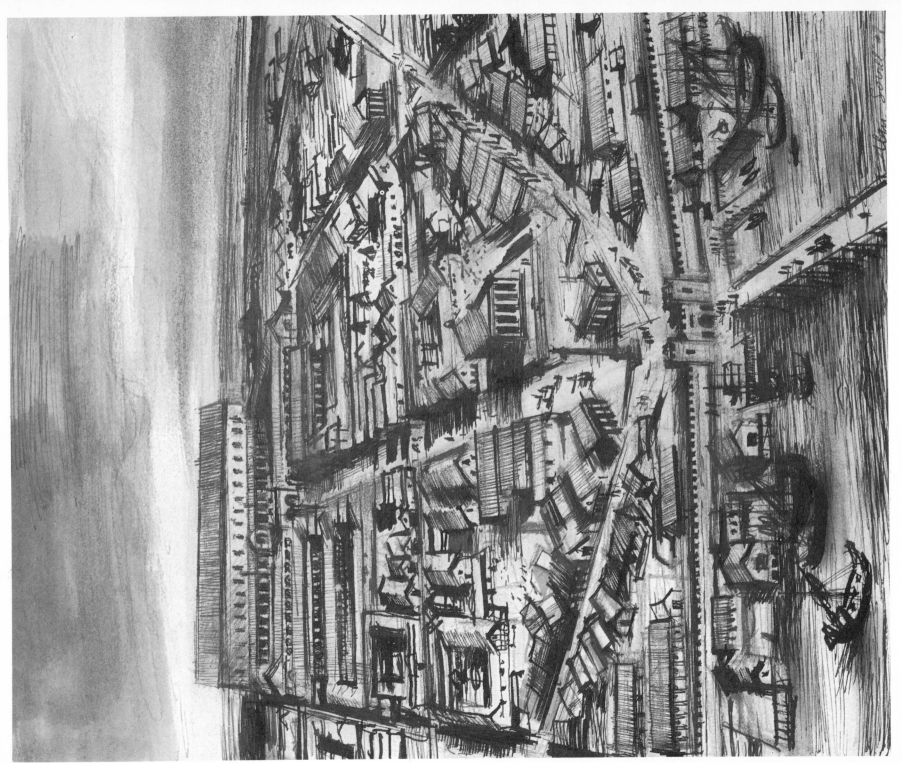

40 *Looking north from the Bridge towards the Forum and Basilica*

41 *Carved stone sarcophagus which enclosed a lead coffin*

In addition the Basilica was the meeting place of the merchants, rather like the Guildhall of 200 years ago. The architectural form of the Basilica, with its aisles separated from the central space, or nave, by rows of columns, and with its apsidal ends, was, of course, the prototype of the early Christian churches of the west.

The Basilica occupied the north side of the great open space of the Forum. They cannot be disassociated, the one from the other, and the Forum might be described as the Atrium or forecourt to the Basilica. Rows of shops and offices were on the south-west and east sides of the Forum, linked and protected by a colonnaded walk. Centrally in the south side there would have been a monumental entrance and in the middle of the square probably a rostrum or an altar flanked by columns crowned by gilded statues. This architectural formality was qualified, no doubt, by the temporary stalls and booths set up on market days and festivals. Archaeological evidence shews that the Forum in its final development dates from Hadrianic times, and substantial traces of its south wall and arcade have been found along the line of Lombard Street where it meets Gracechurch Street. That the building of this Hadrianic Forum made necessary the demolition of earlier buildings of various dates has been demonstrated by the discovery of their fragmentary remains.

42 *The Basilica, showing the north arcade, and the aisle opening on to offices and* ▶
courtrooms. Beyond the cross-wall with the screen of columns is the apsidal east-end
where there would have been a tribune or dais for the delivery of judgments. There is
evidence that the roof was vaulted. Fragments of fresco wall decoration have been
found, and we may reasonably believe the interior to have been as rich and splendid
as it was vast

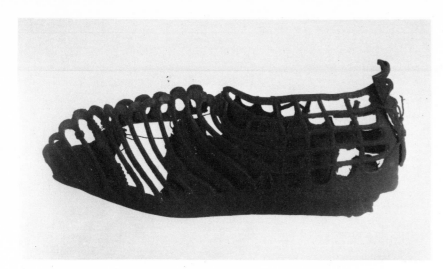

43 *Leather shoe*

The Streets

Traces of a typical Roman grid-pattern of streets have been found in London, and the establishment of this pattern has been greatly helped by the natural assumption that streets led to the gates whose positions were positively established; so an approximately north by south, and east by west grid has been pieced together. But one's instinctive thought in looking back to the very earliest years of the Roman occupation is that, when the legions marching up from the south came over the bridge, they debouched north-west and north-east as well as marching more directly to the north. In other words, there must surely have been an earlier diagonal pattern of roads coming from the bridge, and the typical Roman grid was superimposed on it. But there is very little surviving evidence of this rational plan except for traces of a gravel road on timber foundations running approximately north-west, which does, indeed, exactly conform to the bridge-diagonal pattern. In its presumed direction, based on the evidence of building fragments found at the junction of Bread Lane and Watling Street, it tends to bend towards Ludgate rather than Newgate. To the north-east of the bridge, however, nothing has been discovered which encourages the idea of an Aldgate–Bridge diagonal, so all that can be said is that, whilst some small evidence exists for this rational diagonal plan, there is evidence also for its submergence by the grid-plan. For the latter we have conclusive evidence. From the east end of the Forum, running north to Bishopsgate and Ermine Street, a well-marked length of gravel metalling 25 feet wide has been found made up to no less than eight feet in thickness, which would seem to indicate continual resurfacing over a very long period of time. To the west of the Basilica and Forum indications of another north–south road have been noted, whilst to the south of the Forum, running east and west, and continuing along the line of Bucklersbury, fragments of a well-defined street pointing to Newgate have been unearthed. A portion of this street was found by Sir Christopher Wren when he was digging the foundations for the new church of St Mary-le-Bow after the great fire of 1666. He reported 'a Roman Causeway of rough stone, close and well rammed with Roman Brick and Rubbish at the Bottom,

Alan Sorrell 1947

45 *Wooden writing tablets*

for a Foundation, and all firmly cemented'. So sure was Wren of the stability of this ancient fragment that he laid the foundation of his delicate fantasy of a tower directly upon it. From St Martin le Grand along Newgate Street there are traces of gravel road metalling leading directly to the gate and the road to Silchester and the west. Cannon Street exactly overlies an east–west element in the grid. Walbrook was probably bridged at two points, though no traces of these, presumably timber, structures, have survived. The streets varied in width from 18 to 35 feet. They were made with local gravel mixed with concrete which resulted in an almost rock-like hardness. They were cambered, with gullies along the sides, and they were probably flanked by paved sidewalks, which in some cases may well have been protected by colonnades. The streets were linked by a network of alleys very similar in character to those of medieval London, some of which still survive.

The Walbrook Mithraeum

The discovery of the Walbrook Mithraeum was of such a dramatic and exciting nature that it aroused great public interest, and perhaps more than any other single event has popularised the archaeology of Roman London. This excitement expressed itself in massive slow-moving queues of people who found satisfaction in a brief glance at the foundations of the small ancient building, so soon to be ruthlessly dismembered and uprooted. It had the solemnity of a royal lying-in-state. In 1952 the bombed and rubble-covered Walbrook area now occupied by Bucklersbury House was due for clearance and building development, and Professor Grimes, the then Director of the London Museum, supervised the cutting of exploratory trenches. Great difficulty was experienced in this work because of the water-logged character of the subsoil and the consequent flooding of the trenches. As might have been expected in this main drainage area of the Roman city, a rich haul of metal, pottery and even leather and wooden objects rewarded the investigation, but far outweighing all this in interest and importance was the discovery of the rectangular Temple with its apsidal west end which we now know as the Walbrook Mithraeum, with its superlatively precious content of marble sculptures and the small but very precious silver infuser. (In passing, it may be noted that other fine marble sculptured fragments had been discovered as long ago as 1889 when foundations were dug in the site, without the Temple itself being discovered.) The owners of the site and the builders 'generously undertook to clear the massive modern obstructions' which overlay the site, and the wonderfully perfect remains of the building standing to a height of several feet came to light. The possibility of the presence of archaeological remains on building sites in London and elsewhere must be greatly dreaded by owners and contractors working to a time schedule. In this instance, the uniqueness of the remains and the richness of the marble sculptures found hidden there—hidden presumably from persecuting Christians—and 'without parallel in Britain', to quote Professor Grimes, entitled the Mithraeum to very special consideration. And this it received:

46 The Mithraeum excavations (Prof. Grimes in centre)

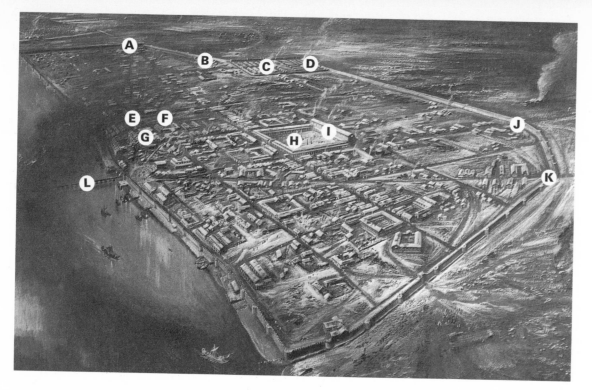

47 *Key to plate 48*

A	Newgate	G	Governor's Palace
B	Aldersgate	H	Forum
C	Fort	I	Basilica
D	Cripplegate	J	Bishopsgate
E	Walbrook	K	Aldgate
F	Mithraeum	L	London Bridge

48 *Roman London in about A.D. 400. The snow-bound city, with burning houses* ▶
beyond the walls, fired by Saxon raiders

49 *The Mithraeum excavations*

there were visits from eminent persons, questions in the House of Commons, and convulsive press publicity.

In what is still a great and rich city, then in the process of not unprofitable recovery from war damage, and with all sorts of vigorous, if generally misdirected schemes of reconstruction taking place, one might have hoped that this discovery would have been cherished and preserved and that a small surrounding green garden oasis might have come into being. It would have become a quiet refuge from the noise and traffic, and a recognition of the ancient roots of the city. The Mithraeum could have been rebuilt and re-roofed, and used as a museum to contain its own treasures. But no, it was all swept away and 'rebuilt' in the office block which superseded it, and so it is today. The cynic might say with some justification that the age is true to itself with commerce supplanting worship. It is thought that the Temple may have been built towards the end of the second century A.D. The presence of an altar base of Constantinian date suggests that it may have become a Christian Church early in the fourth century. Two successive floors sealed the buried Mithraic marbles, proof that the temple continued in use after that act of fear. But there is a surprising footnote to this in the discovery of a marble Bacchic group at a level above what we might call the Christian floor levels. This could mean that the Temple reverted to its original pagan use after an interval as a Christian Church, and this may well have occurred in the short lived revival of paganism under Julian the Apostate (A.D. 360–3).

The Mithraeum was an aisled rectangle which measured 60 feet by 25 feet, with its main axis east and west. At its east end was a cross hall or narthex, whose 'stone door sill, though badly worn was well preserved, with the iron collars for the door pivots still in place' (Grimes). The floor of the narthex was $2\frac{1}{2}$ feet above that of the nave, and wooden steps led down to the latter level. The nave was divided from the aisles by seven columns a side and these columns symbolised 'the seven grades into which the devotees of the cult were divided' (Grimes). The floors of the aisles were raised above the level of the nave, and they were used as benches for the reclining or sitting worshippers. At the west end there was an apse, strongly supported on the outside by massive buttresses. The floor of the apse was like that of the aisles, raised above the nave level. The sculptured relief of Mithras slaying the sacred bull

50 The Walbrook Mithraeum

would have been at the extreme western end of the apse, concealed by a curtain until 'the appropriate times in the ritual' (Grimes). Some sort of tabernacle stood on the straight edge of the apse, and some indications of this were found during the excavations. Towards the eastern end of the nave there were probably two smaller tabernacles containing small statues of Cautopates and Cautes, 'the companions' of Mithras: Cautes holding a torch upwards, symbolising Light, and Cautopates with his torch downwards, Darkness. Small altars, three of which have been found, flanked the nave. At a critical moment in the Mithraic ritual two devotees wearing the fantastic masks and apparel of the Raven and the Lion carried flaming torches. Except for the light coming from very small windows placed high up in the nave wall the services were conducted in darkness tempered only by torchlight, and this deep gloom was intended to emphasise the cave-like feeling of the temple, for Mithras was said to have been 'born from the rocks', and the 'cavern' was used to signify the world.

The Mithraic cult was for a long time a very serious rival to Christianity, and Christian writers unjustly claimed that its ceremonies were a mockery of the True Faith. Mithraism was, in fact, an austere faith with a special appeal to the soldier. The exclusion of women and terrifying ordeals of initiation (it is said there were as many as 80 of these) by heat, cold, brandings, torture and solitude successfully prevented Mithraism from becoming a 'popular' religion. In the Mithraeum's final form the columns were removed by the victorious Christians perhaps because of their ritualistic significance, although as this alteration must have entailed considerable rebuilding and reroofing some more substantial reason may have been present. The floor was also brought to the same level, but the increasingly water-logged condition of the site was sufficient reason for this alteration. It may be noted that Mithraea were normally built where ample water supplies were available for ritualistic purposes, but in the second century the increasing and excessive marshiness of the Walbrook area evidently was not foreseen.

51 Marble head of Mithras from the Mithraeum

52 The Mithraeum: the invocation of the God

53 *East wing of the Governor's Palace*

The Governor's Palace

Cannon Street Station has submerged if not obliterated the western half of a late first-century complex of buildings which have been called, fancifully, but not without some rationality, the 'Governor's Palace'. The recently excavated fragments are bounded on the east by Suffolk Lane, on the south by Upper Thames Street, and on the north by Cannon Street. In a central position on the site are the extremely massive remains of a hall measuring 50 feet by 95 feet, with the longer axis north and south. To the east (and, it is presumed, to the west also) is a fragmentary apsidal structure connected with the central hall by massive walls. To the north and south there were large courtyards enclosed by a quadrilateral of colonnaded buildings comprising a great number of small rooms with indications of staircases which suggest an upper storey. In the south courtyard a great walled pool with its floor six feet below the courtyard level has been identified, with the base of what may well have been a fountain in a rounded projection on its north side—or rather *two* fountains, for bearing in mind the Roman passion for symmetry in architectural form, one may assume that beneath Cannon Street Station lies, or lay, the other complementary half of this Governor's Palace complex. Excavators of the site, whether they have been sewer diggers, railway engineers or archaeologists have commented on the enormously massive construction of the walls: one discovered in 1840 was 20 to 22 feet in width, and when the railway station was being built in 1868 'an immense external wall' 200 feet long, 10 feet high and 12 feet thick running east and west was found, together with cross walls and the remains of apartments with tessellated pavements and wall paintings. The land sloped steeply towards the river in this area, and seems to have been terraced in Roman times, but the courtyards were level, and the south courtyard was built up as a platform of 'flint and ragstone rubble concrete 6–7 feet thick' (Merrifield). Tiles stamped PP.BR.LON. (Procurator Provinciae Britanniae, Londinium) were found and these suggest that they were used in a Government building. The Emperor Hadrian may have stayed in this palace during his visit to Britain in A.D. 122.

54 *The Governor's Palace from the south. The central pilastered feature is aligned in a* ▶ *puzzlingly awkward way. The whole of this suite may have been used for official functions, whilst the buildings around the two courtyards were probably administrative offices and domestic quarters*

The Cemeteries

Under Roman law, burials had to be outside inhabited areas. In towns this meant that cemeteries were generally just beyond the defensive walls, and often they straggled along roads leading to the gates. A traveller approaching a town would therefore pass between ranks of monuments to the dead before reaching the crowded and lively streets. The contrast must have been extraordinary, with the town walls assuming a significance which we cannot fully appreciate today. The London cemeteries were, on the east, between Aldgate and the river. Here was the Classicianus monument, fragments of which are in the British Museum. To the north there was a large cemetery between Bishopsgate and Moorgate, and to the west between St Martin's le Grand and the Fleet River. The law prohibiting burials within the walls appears to have been often broken, and many burial urns and a few coffins have been discovered in the city. In earlier times cremation was the invariable practice, and obviously the concealment of urns containing ashes was easier than in the case of inhumation, and it is likely that in many cases the ashes (after the extra-mural cremation) could remain in the city. But when inhumation began to supersede cremation in the third century, the law-breaking must have been flagrant. The change in custom from cremation to inhumation may indicate the spread of Christianity, with its emphasis on physical resurrection.

55 *The tomb of Classicianus*

64

56 The tomb of Classicianus

The Blackfriars Barge

57 *The Blackfriars Barge as excavated (mast-seating on right)*

The Blackfriars barge was first discovered in 1962—a small portion of the bows—and in the following year another, much larger portion, almost the entire after-part of the craft, was found in the mud to the east of Blackfriars Bridge where the Fleet River once flowed into the Thames. The discovery came about through the forming of a cofferdam in the Thames in connection with roadworks, and this was fortunate since it meant that archaeological investigation could take place in reasonably dry conditions. From the fact that the timbers were found to have been attacked by the teredo beetle, which cannot live in fresh water, it is evident that the barge was not a river craft only, and must have sailed in the salt waters of the estuary, though its shallow build—it was only seven feet to the gunwales—and extremely crude construction makes it unlikely that it ever ventured far from the shelter of the land. Like the traditional Thames barge it was flat-bottomed but, unlike that fine craft, it had no keel and depended on the massiveness of its construction rather than skilful design to enable it to hold together. It is supposed that the barge had a single mast, and the seating of this mast was found. In it was a worn copper coin of Domitian with the reverse of the coin bearing the image of the goddess Fortuna uppermost. There is no evidence to indicate the reason for the foundering of the barge at Blackfriars, but it is thought that the cargo shifted after the barge had sunk, so the idea of a sudden, dramatic heeling-over, with the ragstone splitting its massive sides, can be discounted. The Kentish ragstone cargo has been considered as evidence that this was one of the barges employed to bring the rough stones from the Medway for the building of the city wall between A.D. 193 and 197. The Domitian coin was struck in A.D. 88–89, so that the life of this Blackfriars barge must have been sometime in the second century, ending between 193 and 197. How many times, one wonders, did this clumsy heavy-laden barge creep out of the Medway and drift slowly up the reaches of the Thames, negotiate the bridge and unload its cargo. And how many such barges were involved in this great wall-building operation at Londinium?

58 *The Blackfriars Barge: the confluence of the Fleet with the Thames must have* ▶
caused some difficulty in mooring

Alan Sorrell 13

The Baths in Cheapside

The public bath-house was an important feature of Roman life, and something which with the collapse of the Empire vanished completely from Western Europe, though as the 'Turkish Bath' it survived in the East. Bathing establishments in Roman times were much more than the name suggests, for they were, in addition, places for all kinds of exercise and games, and social and cultural centres. However, in Britain, although important public baths have been discovered at Bath (where the establishment was on a grandiose scale) and at Wroxeter, Leicester and elsewhere, only small-scale bath-houses have been found in London, and perhaps this Cheapside bath suite is the most complete—though lacking palaestra (exercise yard) and apodyterium (undressing room). The site is now covered by the Sun Life Assurance Society building at 100–116 Cheapside. The building was less than 200 yards west of the Walbrook and in a locality where water was abundant, an obviously important consideration in the siting of a building of this kind. The main structure, whose axial line was N.N.E., measured 75 feet by 27 feet with an apsidal projection to the west, a furnace channel to the north, and an extension of undetermined length to the east (this probably contained the apodyterium with the adjacent palaestra). The furnace heated the tepidarium (warm room), caldarium (hot room) and sudatorium or sweating room, by means of hypocausts and wall-flues. The bath ritual ended with a cold plunge. This bath house was probably built in the late first or early second century, was enlarged later in the second century, and appears to have been demolished in the middle of the third century. Bath establishments were looked upon with disfavour by the early Christians who connected them with dissipation, and this disapproval was a reason for their disuse when the Christians obtained power in the early fourth century. In this instance, however, the date assumed for demolition seems a little early for Christian disapproval to have been effective. Probably the increasing marshiness of the site—near enough to the Walbrook to suffer from the rising water level there—was the cause of abandonment. The water tank was, in fact, submerged in black silt, in which were found fragments of second-century pottery.

59 *Flue channel of the Baths in Cheapside*

60 *Roman bath building, Cheapside, looking south. The furnace in the left foreground* ▶ *heated the water in the tank (shown here with a lead roof), which was fed from the cistern on the extreme left. Beyond the warm rooms with the rounded concrete roofs, the tiled portion contained, from left to right, dressing room, plunge bath and cold bath. A Kentish ragstone foundation suggested the likelihood of an open-air swimming bath. Beyond the buildings was an exercise yard, and an arcaded walk and a latrine have been indicated in the drawing.*

68

Acknowledgement

The author is most grateful to the following for their invaluable help in the preparation of this book:

Sir Arthur Young, Commissioner of the City of London Police; Professor W. F. Grimes; Mr Norman Cook, Mr Ralph Merrifield and Mr Peter Marsden, of the Guildhall Museum, London; Dr D. B. Harden and Mr Brian Spencer, of the London Museum; and Mr J. W. Brailsford, of the British Museum.

The author and publishers wish to thank the following for permission to reproduce illustrations appearing in the book:

Aerofilms Ltd for plate 6; the Trustees of the British Museum for plates 1, 8–10, 20, 23, 24, 33, 35, 41, 43, 45 and 55; the City of London Police for plates 22 and 32; the Guildhall Museum, London, for plates 5, 11, 17–19, 27–30, 37, 39, 42, 44, 46, 51, 53, 54 and 57–60; the *Illustrated London News* for plates 26, 50 and 52; the London Museum for plates 2–4, 7, 12–16, 25, 34, 36, 38 and 48; and the Tower Hill Improvement Trust for plate 56.

DATE DUE

MAY 10			
FEB 2 1988			
APR 5 1988			
GAYLORD			PRINTED IN U.S.A.